SLIM GOODBODY'S NUTRITION EDITION

Delicious Dairy

CRABTREE
Publishing Company
www.crabtreebooks.com

Crabtree Publishing Company
www.crabtreebooks.com

Series development, writing, and packaging:
John Burstein, Slim Goodbody Corp.

Editors:
Molly Aloian
Reagan Miller
Mark Sachner, Water Buffalo Books

Editorial director:
Kathy Middleton

Production coordinator:
Kenneth Wright

Prepress technician:
Kenneth Wright

Designer:
Tammy West, Westgraphix LLC

Photos:
Chris Pinchback, Pinchback Photography

Photo credits:
© Slim Goodbody, iStockphotos, and Shutterstock images.

Acknowledgements:
The author would like to thank the following people for their help in this project:
Christine Burstein, Olivia Davis, Kylie Fong, Nathan Levig, Havana Lyman, Andrew McBride, Lulu McClure, Ben McGinnis, Esme Power, Joe Ryan

Library and Archives Canada Cataloguing in Publication

Burstein, John
Delicious dairy / John Burstein.

(Slim Goodbody's nutrition edition)
Includes index.
ISBN 978-0-7787-5041-3 (bound).--ISBN 978-0-7787-5056-7 (pbk.)

1. Dairy products in human nutrition--Juvenile literature.
2. Nutrition--Juvenile literature. I. Title. II. Series:°Burstein, John.
Slim Goodbody's nutrition edition.

QP144.M54B87 2010 j641.3'7 C2009-903853-6

Library of Congress Cataloging-in-Publication Data

Burstein, John.
Delicious dairy / John Burstein.
p. cm. -- (Slim Goodbody's nutrition edition)
Includes index.
ISBN 978-0-7787-5041-3 (reinforced lib. bdg. : alk. paper) -- ISBN 978-0-7787-5056-7 (pbk. : alk. paper)
1. Dairy products in human nutrition--Juvenile literature. 2. Nutrition--Juvenile literature. 3. Children--Nutrition--Requirements--Juvenile literature. I. Title. II. Series.

QP144.M54B87 2010
641.3'7--dc22

2009024559

Crabtree Publishing Company

www.crabtreebooks.com 1-800-387-7650

Published in Canada
Crabtree Publishing
616 Welland Ave.
St. Catharines, Ontario
L2M 5V6

Published in the United States
Crabtree Publishing
PMB16A
350 Fifth Ave., Suite 3308
New York, NY 10118

Published in the United Kingdom
Crabtree Publishing
White Cross Mills
High Town, Lancaster
LA1 4XS

Published in Australia
Crabtree Publishing
386 Mt. Alexander Rd.
Ascot Vale (Melbourne)
VIC 3032

Contents

GREETINGS

My name is Slim Goodbody.
I want to ask you two questions.

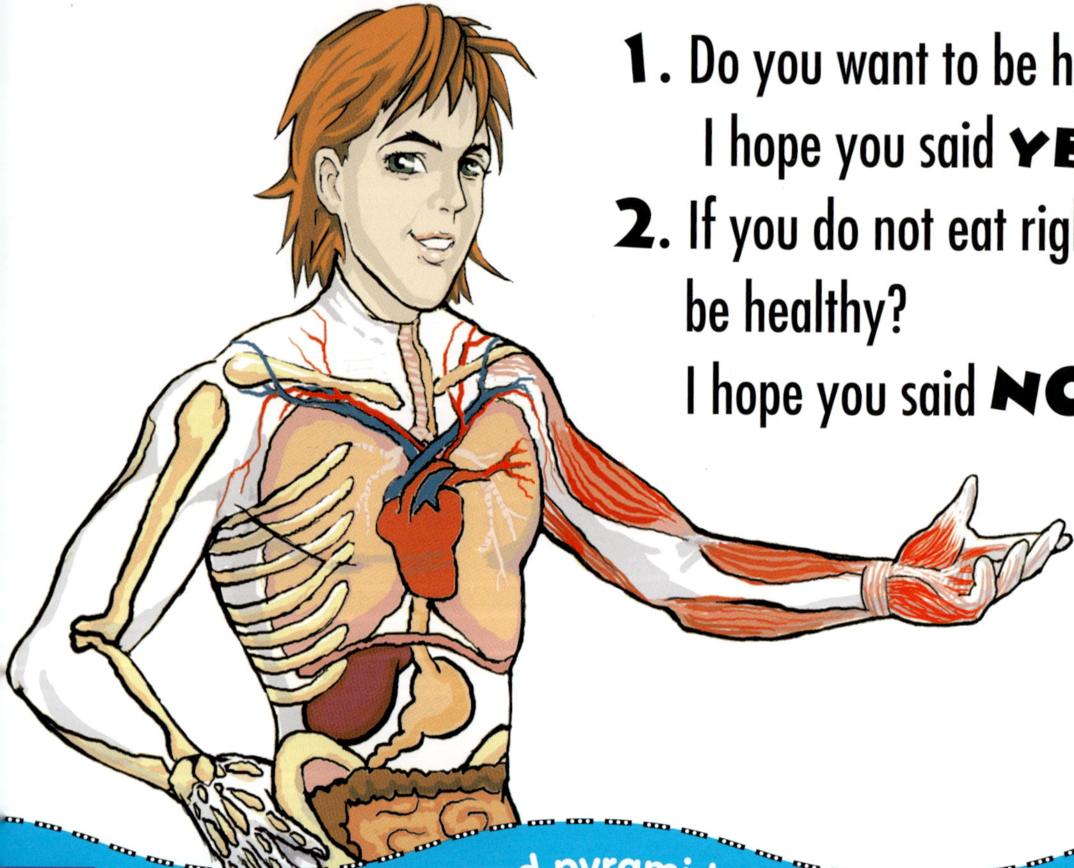

1. Do you want to be healthy?
   I hope you said **YES**.
2. If you do not eat right, can you be healthy?
   I hope you said **NO**.

The food pyramid helps you eat right.

There are six stripes on the U.S. food pyramid.

The stripes stand for the five different food groups plus oils.

GRAINS
VEGETABLES
FRUITS
OILS
MILK
MEAT
& BEANS

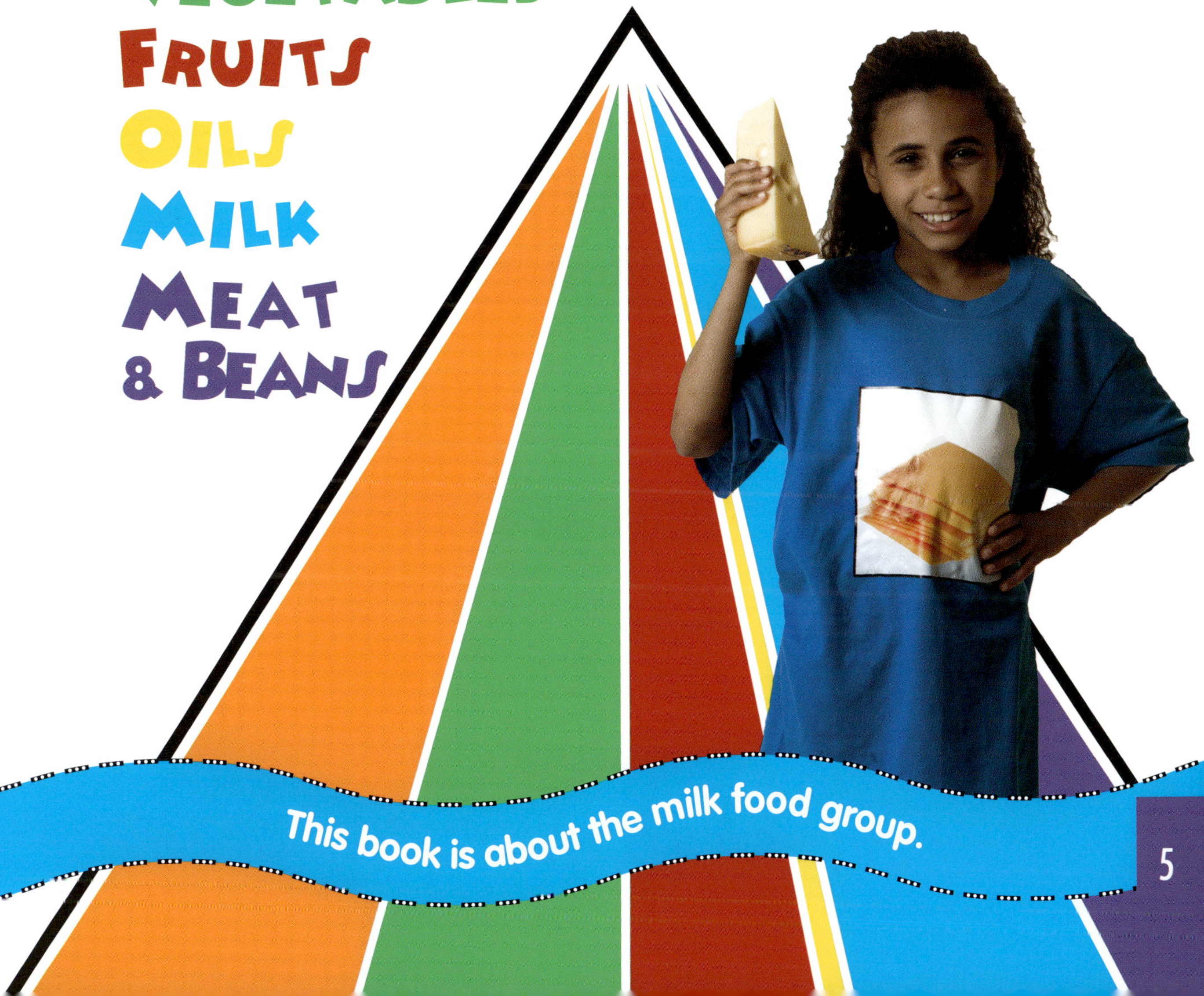

This book is about the milk food group.

Milk!

The milk group belongs on the blue stripe in the U.S. food pyramid. The milk group includes milk and foods made with milk.

Low-fat or fat-free milk is best.

American cheese

cheddar cheese

yogurt

swiss cheese

cottage cheese

pudding

ice cream

COW TO CARTON

I think it is amazing
How milk in your glass
Starts out in a field,
With a cow munching grass.

She happily chomps
All her sweet grassy greens,
Until she is led
To the milking machines.

Her lovely sweet milk
Is pumped into a vat.
The farmer says "thank you"
And gives her a pat.

The milk in the vat
Is kept cold as can be.
Then a truck drives it off
To a milk factory.

And soon it is ready
To gurgle and pour
Into bottles and cartons
You buy at the store.

It takes milk about two days to get from the cow to the store.

AROUND THE WORLD

In North America, most of our milk comes from cows.

Around the world, other animals give people milk as well.

Milk Keeps You Healthy

Milk helps keep you healthy.

The milk group helps different body parts.

Milk helps your
eyes see well.

Milk helps your
bones grow strong.

Milk gives your muscles
energy to move.

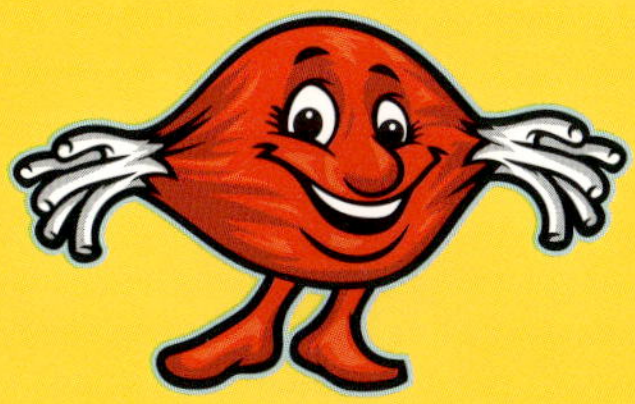

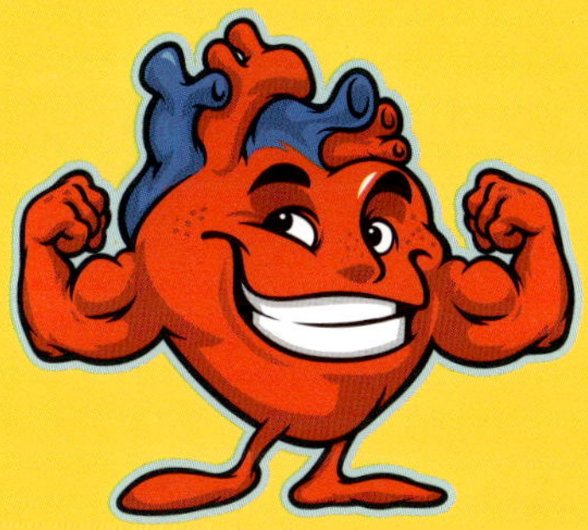

Milk helps your
heart pump well.

Milk helps your
teeth stay hard.

You Need Milk Each Day

You need two cups (500 ml) of milk everyday.

Choose fat-free or low-fat yogurt and cheese.

You can use this list to help you get the milk you need.

Here is what counts as 1 cup:

- 1 half-pint container of milk
- 1 cup of yogurt
- 2 cups of cottage cheese
- 3 slices of processed cheese
- 2 slices of hard cheese
- 1 cup of pudding
- 1 cup of frozen yogurt
- 3 scoops of ice cream

1 cup = 250 ml

Any Time

Almost any time is a good time for milk.

You can have yogurt at breakfast time.

You can drink milk with your lunch.

You can snack on some cheese after school.

You can have some pudding after dinner for dessert.

You can have a frozen yogurt treat on a hot summer day.

MILK TROUBLES

Many people cannot drink milk that comes from cows. Even if they eat foods made with cow's milk, their tummies hurt.

Cow's milk contains a type of sugar called lactose.

These people drink other kinds of milk. They drink soy milk, rice milk, or lactose-free milk.

Lactose can make some people feel sick.

Holy Cow!

Only mother cows can give milk.
A cow must have a calf once a year to keep milking.

A grown-up cow can weigh about 1,400 pounds (635 kilograms).

A newborn calf can weigh about 100 pounds (45 kilograms).

In 1611, Pilgrims first brought cows to America.

In one day, one cow gives enough milk for 100 people to have a glass.

A cow spends six to seven hours a day eating.

A cow drinks about a bathtub full of water per day.

Cows have no upper front teeth.

No two cows have exactly the same pattern of spots.

World Food Guides

The U.S. food pyramid is only one guide to eating well.

To learn more about Canada's Food Guide, check out the Web site below.

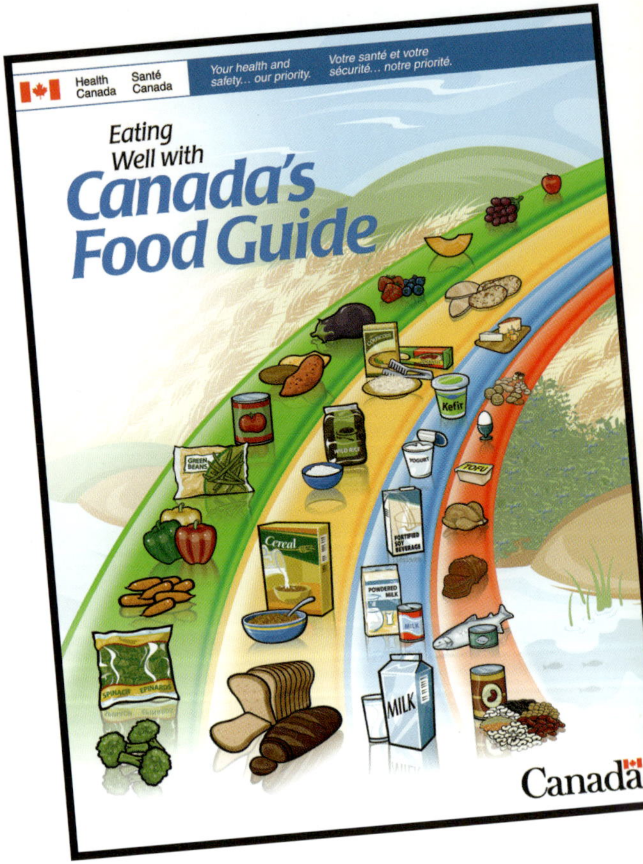

www.nms.on.ca/Elementary/canada.htm

People from different parts of the world often eat different kinds of foods. People use different food guides to help them eat wisely.

Every day, everyone, everywhere needs milk.

Words to Know

container

soy milk

vat

water buffalo

yaks

yogurt

Find Out More

Books

The Milk Makers, Gail Gibbons, Aladdin.

Milk: From Cow to Carton, Aliki, HarperCollins.

Web Sites

MyPyramid.gov
www.mypyramid.gov/kids/index.html

Slim Goodbody
www.slimgoodbody.com

Printed in the U.S.A.-CG